The Small Agency's Guide to Winning New Business

8 Steps to Winning More of the Right Kinds of Clients

JODY SUTTER

ISBN-13: 978-1986008037
ISBN-10: 1986008037

DEDICATION

This book is dedicated to my clients—past, present and future.
May you all be in control of your new business destiny.

CONTENTS

ACKNOWLEDGMENTS

I do for others what they can't do for themselves. That's a two-way street, of course. I want to acknowledge the important role my own business coach, FF, and the community she's created played in inspiring me to write this book.

INTRODUCTION

"I just need more leads in my sales pipeline."

When I hear those words, I know I'm talking to an agency CEO that either doesn't need me, or doesn't *realize* she needs me.

We all want our pipelines filled.

Or, better stated, we'd all rather not have sales pipelines at all!

Imagine a world where clients find you without resistance, willingly pay your fees, and are perfect collaborators over the term of a long and happy relationship?

The reality is more a feast-and-famine cycle of too much work (and not always with the ideal kinds of clients) and then scarcity (sometimes sudden). During the busy parts of the cycle, it's easy to get lulled into a sense of complacency, or to convince yourself that business development isn't a priority compared to keeping your current clients happy (even if they are making you miserable).

I've both lived and witnessed this cycle so many times that talking about it here seems like stating the obvious. And yet, the problem is chronic. I continually get calls from agency CEOs asking me to end all their problems by filling their pipeline.

Full disclosure: that was my mission when I first started The Sutter Company. I was going to do the job that most agency leaders found difficult and even distasteful: lead generation.

You see, I had been one of those rare agency business development pros who actually had a background in sales. Any hesitation about pitching to strangers was extinguished a long time ago. In my new company, I would take on the role that no one else seemed to want. Clients would flock to me. My pipeline would be perpetually filled.

In fact, it wasn't hard to find prospective clients for my budding business. What *was* hard was making any kind of difference for them. My business model was broken because more often than not, my ad agency clients lacked a compelling offer.

This is not to say that these agencies weren't staffed with creative, smart, ambitious people, or that they hadn't done outstanding work for their blue-chip clients. They were and they had.

So what?

For every one of my clients, there were dozens of others that could also lay claim to a talented team, excellent client work, and an attractive client roster.

And they all wanted full pipelines too.

After the first few frustrating assignments, I realized that my success as a lead generator hinged on my ability to tell a great story over time. It often takes multiple tries over the course of months to nurture a prospect to the point they want to meet with you, much less work with you.

I began interviewing my prospective clients, asking them:

- What are you selling?

- Who are you selling it to?

- How are you selling it?

Simple questions. Deceptively difficult to answer.

And, when the answers didn't come easily (or, just as telling, when the answer did come easily, but it sounded like everyone else's vague, buzz-wordy pitch), that was my signal that, should the agency hire me, I would fail.

Unless…

What if I helped them to answer those questions? Then I'd equip myself with the ammunition I needed to effectively generate leads.

At the same time, I had another epiphany.

These small agency CEOs, who were (and still are) the majority of my clients, *were the best business development resource their agency had.*

Why?

Quite simply, they were the ones who had the most at stake. They're the hungriest. They're the ones who will go without a paycheck first if business dries up.

They're also the agency's most passionate boosters. I hate seeing the word "passion" being used (or over-used) by agencies in describing their culture or approach. It sounds empty to me – except when describing the CEO.

And, CEOs, especially if they're owners and/or founders, tend to have an entrepreneurial mindset. They hustle. They do what they need to do to grow the business.

What if I could help these leaders control their agency's new business destiny without having to rely on third-party lead generation firms?

What if I could even help them discover their unique business development mojo? Then I could help them develop a new business strategy and plan that relies less on chaos and more on focus, one that is easier to embrace and sustain. A strategy that makes sense *for them*.

That's what I hope this book will do for you. It won't be the last book you read on how to grow your business, but it will get you started on a path toward the kind of sustainable business development practices that are right for your agency.

1 IF YOU'RE NOT CLEAR ABOUT WHAT YOU DO, NO ONE ELSE IS EITHER

Quick, what's your agency's unique selling proposition? What's your elevator pitch?

If you're like a lot of the agency CEOs I work with, you stumbled to come up with the answer.

Or, maybe you stated the answer confidently, but the answer sounded something like this:

> *"We're a full-service, integrated agency. What makes us unique is our team of talented brand storytellers who always put the client first."*

Yeah, you and about 120,000 other agencies in North America.[1]

You deserve to be noticed!

But you need to do your part too. You're responsible for making it as easy as possible for your best customers to find you.

---

[1] The approximate number of North American agencies according to agency search database provider Agency Spotter. Agency Spotter takes a broad view and includes everything from digital agencies, PR firms, design studios, and research firms.

This hit home for me recently when I got a phone call from one of my clients, the CEO of a small ad agency, to tell me that the agency's positioning strategy, a strategy that I first suggested more than three years earlier and have encouraged (and sometimes cajoled) him to embrace ever since, just won him a major piece of business.

Committing to that positioning strategy had been a psychological hurdle. It fit like a Savile Row suit, but it required him to put a stake in the ground, and that meant potentially saying "no" to revenue if it meant working with the wrong kinds of clients.

And what are the wrong kinds of clients? Clients you work with only for the money, that don't respect your expertise, and do nothing towards furthering the vision you have for your agency.

Look, you don't *have to* have an airtight positioning strategy. Plenty of agencies stumble along without one.

But, when you do, everything about business development gets easier:

- It informs your ideal client profile
- It anchors your point-of-view and shapes a content marketing strategy
- It guides you toward the right decisions about whether to pitch an account or pass
- You'll be confident in the value you offer
- Your team will be more invested and less burnt-out
- You'll make pitch presentations that are more focused and persuasive

Now that you're convinced, where do you start?

You start with the basics:

What are you selling? As basic as it gets, what's the thing people most want to buy from you? Brand strategy? Creative ideas? Media buying? SEO?

Who are you selling to? How do you define your ideal kind of client?

My challenge to you is to get this down to a simple equation:

"We do [service you provide] for [clients you provide it to]."

For example,

"We specialize in Facebook ad campaigns for auto dealerships."

"We develop social media strategies for hospitality businesses."

"We provide strategic digital solutions for progressive nonprofits."

Now, compare that to:

"We're a full-service agency for Fortune 5000 clients."

Being clear about what you do and who you serve has two more benefits: it will save you time and money.

On average, small to midsized agencies spend **$450,000** a year preparing for pitch meetings. That's according to a study conducted in late 2015 by consumer insights firm CubeYou.[2]

These agencies reported that they pitch about ten new clients a year and the average investment per final pitch meeting, in real and third-party costs, was $45,000 (and that's not including the cost at the RFP stage, which was $15,000 per RFP).

---

[2] 7 Stats You Didn't Know About Pitching: http://blog.cubeyou.com/how-top-agencies-win-over-75-of-their-new-business-pitches

Pitching is *expensive*. And the more general your focus, the more money and time you'll need to invest to support it.

Here's why:

- Generalists seek out clients; specialists are sought
- Generalists are forced to differentiate based on price; specialists can afford to charge a premium
- Generalists will always be tempted to reinvent themselves to suit the nature of the prospect; specialists will find it easier to home in on a consistent message that's effective for the right audience

When it comes to business development, generalists are inefficient; specialists are efficient.

For all you full-service agencies out there, *look at this less like a stark choice between one side or the other and more as shifting the cost-to-benefit ratio in your favor.*

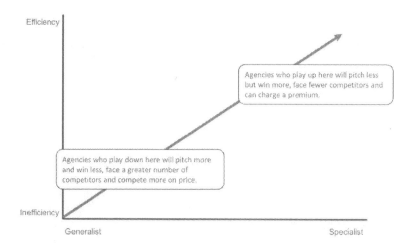

If all those good things await, what's holding some agencies back?

I've narrowed it down to three obstacles:

1. Emotion

Finding the right positioning for your agency can be emotional, soul-searching work, and emotion tends to cloud our judgment and compromise our objectivity. We may put in long hours of concerted effort and serious discussion and still end up with a vague and ineffective result

2. Fear

By its nature, positioning your agency in the marketplace limits the number of potential clients that are going to be right for your agency.

It's easy to misinterpret that to mean that you'll be limiting your opportunity to generate revenue, which seems like scary stuff. In fact, the opposite is true.

3. Abstraction

Our business deals in abstractions.

I don't deny that the outcomes produced are visual, aural or tactile units of marketing, but the real value of what we do is abstract and intangible. Abstract concepts are hard to describe, much less place a value on.

You can address these obstacle by seeking outside perspectives from experts like me, but I'll be the first to tell you that my job is to guide you, not hand you the answers.

In other words, outside perspective helps you navigate around these dangerous obstacles, but it shouldn't design your ship.

Fortunately, there are strategies you can use to remove (or diminish) all three of these obstacles and guide you toward clear answers to those three simple questions that are deceptively difficult to answer:

What are you selling?

Who are you selling it to?

How are you selling it?

2 QUIETING EMOTIONS

What if you had a way to test your positioning that puts emotion to the side?

When I work with an agency on its positioning, we test our hypotheses against this checklist. We ask, is the positioning:

Succinct?

Targeted?

Repeatable?

Accurate?

Flexible?

Differentiated?

Is it succinct?

Remember the equation from the last chapter:

"We do [service you provide] for [clients you provide it to]."

It's simple and complete. One sentence. It's that easy.

But, positioning statements are often an unwieldy sequence of jargon, generalizations and overblown adjectives. What's more, in the pursuit of clarity, many agencies try to pile more on top of their already overburdened statement rather than paring it down to essentials.

Of course, not all succinct positioning statements are effective. "We're a full-service advertising agency serving a range of consumer marketers" is certainly succinct, but it tells your prospective clients little.

Luckily the rest of the checklist offsets that.

Is it targeted?

One measure of a strong positioning statement is when the target audience can recognize itself in it.

Here's an example: "Industrial Strength Marketing: We are a full-service agency that solves marketing challenges for manufacturers, distributors and logistics." (And the agency's website, http://marketstrong.com, pays it off.)

This one sentence does a lot of heavy lifting on behalf of its agency. By simply appearing prominently on its website, it instantly prequalifies prospective customers. If you're not a manufacturer, you're the wrong kind of client.

For the agency, it eliminates all the time it takes to have a qualifying call or a meeting with the client and then the necessary internal discussion that follow about whether to proceed or not.

Is it repeatable?

A lot of positioning strategies are way too complicated. It's usually symptomatic of trying to be all things to all people, which is a desire driven by fear (to be addressed in the next chapter).

A good positioning should be easy for anyone to understand and repeat.

That goes first and foremost for your employees, especially those responsible for new business. I've witnessed numerous situations where an enthusiastic and well-meaning new business person fails to live up to expectations because she wasn't given the right ammunition to begin with.

But it also goes for prospective clients. Information that's easily repeatable is also easy to remember. You want your prospects to remember you beyond that first call or meeting, right?

When you saddle your audience with a fussy positioning statement that's hard to remember and awkward to say, it loses its utility and it rarely gets used.

Is it accurate?

Why would an agency want an inaccurate positioning strategy?

And yet I see it all the time, often in the form of aspirational statements like "We're the agency positioned for the digital future."

OK, I just made that one up, but I wouldn't be surprised if there's an agency out there that's staked that claim. To be fair, it might even be true, but usually it describes what an agency *wants to be* and not what it is.

If it's not accurate, then how do you prove it? Either you don't, and your argument falls apart once you start taking your prospective client through your case studies, or you obfuscate (maybe not intentionally) with overblown adjectives like "passionate" and "relentless" or phrases like how you "live and breathe" branding or social media or whatever it is you want to prove that you do.

Aspiring is a good thing but make it a part of your internal communications strategy or the annual management offsite instead.

Is it flexible?

This might seem like I'm reversing myself a bit but having an element of flexibility in your positioning strategy can be a good thing.

It's like a foundation for the structure you want to build. It grows with you, but it becomes shaky if it's asked to support something that it wasn't designed to support.

Is it differentiating?

I hate to break it to you, but an "obsession with getting business results" does not make you unique.

With more than 120,000 agencies in North America, differentiating your agency from competitors is *hard*. But I think uniqueness has less to do with a singular, own-able quality and more to do with how those qualities are arranged.

It's like DNA – we're all made up of the same stuff, and yet none of us are the same.

Once you realize this, you're in a better position to survey the full range of qualities that describe your agency. When you first embark on this exercise, try not to edit and don't take the obvious stuff for granted. I've often seen a special magic happen when a handful of what seems to be pedestrian qualities are brought together to form something compelling.

You have a choice. You can choose the path of least differentiation, but it may increase your costs of business development and decrease your level of competitiveness.

Is it polarizing?

Does your positioning offer a polarizing point of view?

This is scary territory for a lot of ad agencies because it forces them to question a long-held belief in services businesses that the client is always right.

Having a polarizing point of view means people won't always agree with you. Some of those people might be prospects, but they also probably fall into the "wrong client" category.

Of course, your polarizing point of view, if you have one, must be authentic and shouldn't be designed to offend. What it will do is attract the believers. It will also prequalify your leads, weeding out those that want to base their decision on price rather than expertise.

3 STARING DOWN FEAR

You are selling stuff every day, whether it's convincing your team to try new collaboration software or coaxing your kids to eat breakfast.

Selling puts you in a vulnerable position. There's always a risk that you'll fail to persuade the other party to buy.

When it comes to your kids or your team, you've got the leverage of your authority on your side.

When it comes to a prospective client, you've got the leverage of your expertise. The problem is, in many cases, the client doesn't know that yet. To them, you're just one of dozens of agencies that she's already heard from this week, none of which did a persuasive job of convincing her it was worth her time to meet them.

We don't like feeling vulnerable or being rejected. In fact, it's a deeper feeling than dislike. It usually comes closer to straight-up fear.

To avoid the fear, we might convince ourselves to stay in our safe place and keep doing whatever it is we've been doing (or not doing), no matter how unsatisfying or unproductive it is.

The devil you know…

Here are four fears that get in the way of committing to a business development plan of action and some strategies to address them.

Fear of missing out on revenue

This is likely the most common fear I hear from agency owners:

> *"If I narrow down my potential customers I might miss out on revenue opportunities."*

Revenue from any source is compelling when you've got payroll to make, but you usually pay in other ways when that revenue is from the wrong kinds of clients.

The first thing to think realistically about is how many revenue opportunities you can pursue at one time and how much work you can afford to invest in those efforts. If you're running a small agency in which each leader (including you) wears many hats, you need to be selective in how you allocate your time to stay profitable and keep existing clients happy.

Plus, when you're selective about what new business you pursue, it's easier to tailor your sales pitch and your marketing messages to that narrower audience. It has the effect of prequalifying prospects so that by the time they come to you with a real opportunity, it's likely you'll work less and close deals more.

I also remind clients that serving a targeted market and attracting clients outside of that market are not necessarily mutually exclusive. If you're a busy firm serving the luxury housewares market, for example, and a spirits brand knocks on your door, there's no reason you can't answer.

However, once you see how rewarding doing business from a focused position can be, you may find yourself turning those clients away. Opportunities outside of your zone of genius can dilute your focus and distract your team, devaluing what you offer.

Fear your team will be unmotivated

The next most common fear I encounter is the fear that saddling your team with work from within the same category or discipline will render them unmotivated, which will torpedo morale and prompt some of them to polish up their résumés.

You're in the services business, therefore you require a happy, motivated team to churn out your product. But, if you shape your business based on what motivates your team rather than the value you provide to the marketplace, you end up trapped.

An all-things-to-all-people new business strategy is inefficient, which means that keeping your team happy may entail more time and money than you can afford to spend. Eventually, your talent pool will become disgruntled and/or dissatisfied, so you're going to lose them anyway.

You have to step outside this sticky issue to solve it. You have to go back to figuring out what kind of agency you want to run. You can still have a happy, motivated team that works in one discipline or category – I know because I've seen them – it just may not be the same team you have right now.

Fear of new patterns in your business

Noticing new patterns in your new business cycle can be alarming, especially if those patterns don't look so rosy.

Here's an example. For the first decade or more of the 21st century, unbridled growth was the norm for a lot of small digital agencies. Digital advertising was a powerful yet unknown force for many marketers. They scrambled to find qualified experts who could help them.

Demand exceeded the supply. Life was good.

As with any market trend, things leveled off and there came a day when the flow of inquiries from prestigious marketers started to ebb. Supply caught up with demand and these agencies were faced with something they never had to do before—actively pursue new business.

This is daunting stuff, especially if it contrasts with a decade during which little effort had to be made to get new clients and grow revenue.

Even though these agencies were masters of a new form of advertising, they faced classic business development challenges that can only be addressed by getting back to the basics:

- Figuring out the agency's ideal client profile(s)
- Getting the positioning and marketing message right
- Setting up systems to ensure new business efforts are more efficient than chaotic

Fear of being an imposter

I was talking to a former agency owner recently about new business and he surprised me by saying that "imposter syndrome" would sometimes get in his way.

Imposter syndrome, for those who aren't familiar with it or have been lucky enough never to experience it, describes an inability to internalize one's accomplishments resulting in a fear of being exposed as a "fraud."

I'd never considered the effects of imposter syndrome on new business, but it made so much sense, especially when I thought about the smaller agencies I work with where business development is led by the CEO, not a dedicated biz dev expert.

Feeling like a fraud is a pretty powerful de-motivator.

The antidote is to get comfortable with stepping into your role as an expert. Sounds easier said than done, but it starts with a simple shift.

I do an exercise with my clients designed to initiate that shift.

When I first tried it in one of my workshops, I was more than anxious (I'm not immune to imposter syndrome myself). It came on the heels of another exercise that explored the qualities that could differentiate the agency from its competitors. That exercise was agonizing for them.

But, once the focus was taken off them, they were freed of self-doubt and the answers flowed. We were left with dozens of insights that could be converted into compelling sales or marketing messages. Now, stepping more confidently into the role of an expert didn't seem so farfetched.

So that's one strategy – stop making it about you and make it about them – or, rather, what you know about them, which is probably substantial.

Get comfortable with the idea that your knowledge is valuable to your prospective clients. When you begin to doubt, make a list of at least 20 things that you know about them – their category, the way they're structured, their business cycle.

You've solved numerous marketing challenges for them by harnessing your expertise.

Own it.

4 DEFEATING ABSTRACTION

Marketing is a craft that relies on abstract thought processes that lead to inspirational ideas like "Just do it."

The problem is, abstract ideas are difficult to describe and even more difficult to value. "Just do it." means little without the context of Nike, the brand which it's served so well for so long.

No doubt there are those of you whose output is more tangible than others, however I'd argue that the real value of what you do lies less in the final outcome and more in the road you took to get there—the poring over the research, the process of getting to know your client, the messy and unpredictable way you arrived at a great creative or strategic idea.

We can unreel it even further and include the collective experience of your team, the methods you use to recruit the best talent, and even your corporate values (assuming they're more than just words on your website or the wall behind the reception desk).

Still not convinced?

Think about how often you search for the right way to describe the work you do only to succumb to meaningless, anemic phrases.

Maybe you're not even aware you do it, but most of you do.

Here's a quick experiment I did. I randomly choose four digital agencies from a list of attendees at a recent conference. Only one of them had a clear, compelling message about what they do and who they serve on the home page of their website.

Here's what the others said (agency names removed to protect the guilty):

> [Agency] embraces the humanity in business to build brands that have emotional resonance. We're more than a global business-to-business marketing agency. We're a movement that's changing the way technology companies view themselves, their customers, and the world.

> Marketing tailored to you. Your vision got you this far. Our strategies honor your core values and mission. We elevate your business and never lose sight of your foundations.

> We integrate technology and humanity. We are an experience design and technology agency that transforms businesses. Our teams unite people, processes, and technology to create human-centered digital experiences. Our approach will change how you think about agencies, operations, and outcomes.

And the fourth agency:

> Strategic digital solutions for progressive nonprofits.

Phew. I feel like I can finally exhale...

Agencies have a hard time describing what it is they do and why it's valuable to a client. It doesn't matter if the agency is big or small, new or decades old, design or digital.

It's a pervasive problem because your value, that is, the reason why a client is willing to pay you money, lies in the abstract stuff of your ideas and how you got to them. And it's difficult to describe intangible, abstract ideas and processes in tangible ways, much less communicate their value.

That's what is truly important to the client. The final product – and the business outcomes that were a result of it – are important evidence but the journey tells your client so much more.

What's the solution?

First, take a critical look at your own brand message and be willing to admit that you might be guilty of the same sins of jargon, wordiness and generalizations as your peers are.

How much is this helping you to attract the right kinds of clients? You all sound the same (even if it is indecipherable at times) and there are hundreds of thousands of you.

There's a technique for breaking this bad habit and all of us already have what it takes to master it: storytelling.

Your compelling story is unique to you. You may share experiences and capabilities with others, but your journey is singular.

And your clients want to hear the story of that journey. Why?

First, because they can't help themselves. As you'll see in the next chapter, we humans are hardwired to engage when we're being told a story.

Second, because it puts all that indecipherable, repetitive information into a format we can absorb and react to in a critical way.

From the client's perspective, this means they finally have a way to compare one agency to the other. They can justify their decision for selecting an agency because the agency's story backs up its claims.

An agency that masters storytelling no longer has to rely on meaningless terms like relentless, innovative or "consumer at the core" because the stories offer proof instead.

5 STORYTELLING IS SELLING

Effective salespeople know that a good story is the fastest route between them and winning new business.

Why?

For one thing, stories are easy to remember.

Chip and Dan Heath illustrated that point in the first few pages of their book *Made to Stick* with the example of an urban legend known as "the kidney heist." For those of you who know the story[3], how many times did you need to hear it before you could repeat it yourself?

My guess is that once did the trick. Maybe you missed some of the finer points, but you were able to get the general idea across.

Now think about the last new business pitch you gave or prospecting email you sent. Did it have the same effect?

---

[3] For those who don't know this urban legend, here's the plot in broad strokes: A man/woman travels out of town on business and hooks up with a stranger, who ends up drugging them. They wake up hours later in a tub of ice to find stitched up incisions on their side where their kidneys are located. These strangers steal the kidney to sell on the black market for transplants. There are a lot of variations of the tale, but they always contain these same points.

To be fair, the kidney heist is filled with the kind of lurid details we humans love but that have no place in a new business pitch. But the other thing that the kidney heist has going for it is that it's a story – and stories have a completely legitimate role to play in winning you more new business.

They give your prospective clients, who may know almost nothing about you, something to relate to. Stories make it easier for them to remember you and to repeat to others what they liked about you.

This is not just my personal theory. Science backs this up.

Neuroscientists have conducted research that reveals our brains are hard-wired to engage when we're being told a story.[4] In fact, storytelling is essential for us to process raw data into information we can act on.

You write stories all day, every day

You're in the business of telling great stories:

VW "Think Small."

Apple "Get a Mac"

Dove "Real Beauty"

And, of course Nike "Just do it"

You just need to learn how to tell them about yourself.

What makes a great story?

Storytelling is the perfect persuasion tool and you have the innate ability to use it.

All good stories, from the mundane to the sublime, have these elements in common:

---

[4] For more reading on this, see *Story Proof: The Science Behind the Startling Power of Story* by Kendall Haven.

- A beginning, a middle and an end
- A protagonist—a primary actor propelling the story forward
- Something at stake—money, love, the preservation of the human race
- Surprises and setbacks—events that draw us in and make us root for an outcome

While storytelling is a technique that novelists, playwrights and others have spent lifetimes perfecting, the basics are easy to grasp. They're as innate in us as language.

When I work with ad agencies to help them communicate more effectively with prospects, I start by showing them the stories that surround them just waiting to be told—client successes, the team's experience, the decisions made and struggles overcome to build an agency into what it is today.

Often these stories are taken for granted, either because they're treated as table stakes or because the agency is simply too close to them to recognize their value. The irony is that agencies replace these simple but powerful narratives with familiar, empty phrases or bulleted lists, both of which have the opposite effect than the one they've intended.

For example, in case study results, I see a tendency to rely on lots of big sounding numbers and percentages at the expense of anecdotes about, say, a clever negotiating approach or unexpected setbacks that were successfully overcome.

It's not that big increases in revenue or engagement aren't important; it's that the reader must work harder to process that information into a narrative they can digest. Essentially, in your effort to impress, you're putting up a roadblock between you and the business you want to win.

Where to start?

Even if I've convinced you that being human is the only qualification you need to master storytelling, you may still be wondering how to harness your natural talent.

Case studies are a great place to start.

By their nature, they have all the elements of a good story:

- The form is the same: challenge + solution + results is equivalent to a story's beginning, middle and end
- A protagonist, which may be the client or the brand or your agency's team.
- There's revenue and reputation at stake—both for you and your client.
- And, unless someone out there can prove to me they've mastered a frictionless creative process, there are always surprises and setbacks.

Like I said earlier, the surprises and setbacks are what make the story so interesting. They tell your prospect what you want them to know—that you're perseverant, innovative, relentless, client-focused, committed to your work—without having to rely on those empty-sounding phrases.

You make it easy for the prospect to understand your value, to relate to you, and to remember and repeat to others what they like about you and why they want to hire you.

Good stories are often short stories.

As you start to trust your storytelling capacity, try using it in more challenging formats, like a prospecting email or a tweet. Trust me, all the elements of a good story can be packed into 280 characters or less.

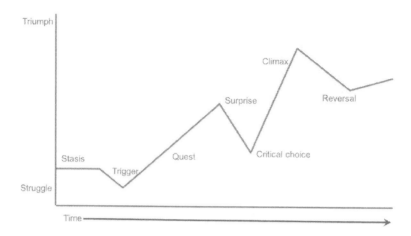

An example of a classic story arc

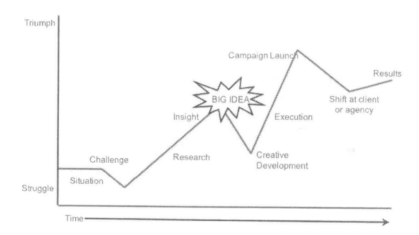

The classic story arc aligns beautifully with the format of a case study

Need more proof?

Ernest Hemingway once bet that he could write a six-word short story that could make people cry. The wager was ten dollars, which Hemingway won with the following:

For sale: Baby shoes. Never worn.

I hope your stories will never be as tragic, but they can make a similar impact. Trust your innate ability to connect with your prospects who are, after all, other humans who just want to hear a good story.

6 YOUR NEW BUSINESS STRENGTHS PROFILE

Have you ever found yourself in a position of being forced to do something you felt you weren't suited to do?

My life partner has a small 4-seater airplane, a Piper Cherokee, in which we make occasional trips to Newport or Boston, or even an impromptu flight to Block Island for dinner on a summer evening.

He thought it would be a great idea for me to be a pilot too, and I didn't disagree. How cool would that be to have two pilots in the family?

After my first flying lesson, the answer to that question was, "not cool at all."

I'm not afraid of flying—in fact I love being a passenger—but I was surprisingly petrified sitting in the pilot's chair. I was overwhelmed by all the information a pilot is required to juggle and, what's worse, I found it all pretty uninteresting.

Fear and boredom – not a good combination.

Some people feel the same when confronted with business development responsibilities at their agencies.

After years of extolling the virtues of a well-rounded business development program, I finally realized that I was never going to get different agency leaders to do things they didn't like to do.

Instead, the shortest, most efficient way to fill their pipelines was to build a program of tactics that aligned well with their talents and internal resources.

I started to figure that out by looking at the new business personalities and proclivities of each agency I worked with.

Four types emerged:

- Hunters
- Promoters
- Communicators
- Thinkers

Hunters

Hunters have an instinct for selling. They're energized by making connections with other people and feel at ease when interacting with strangers, whether on the phone or in person.

Most agencies are not filled with natural-born hunters, which is why they usually fail to sustain any sort of plan that entails outbound prospecting. Neither carrots nor sticks seem to make much of a difference with these teams. I've seen financial incentives and promises of career advancement fail in equal measure.

For the few of you whom this *does* describe, you'll probably want to set up systems and a structure to support a prospecting plan. Don't forget to establish the basics first:

- What are you selling and who are you selling it to?
- Do you have a well-maintained arsenal of tools (case studies, your website, testimonials, social media streams) to back that up?

Promoters

These are leaders with big personalities (and often big egos too) who've got something to say and aren't afraid to say it. Often their business life bleeds into their personal life, and vice versa.

A great example of a Promoter is Gary Vaynerchuk.[5] Vaynerchuk is the ultimate ambassador for Vayner Media, the company that bears his name. He practices what his agency preaches, boasting more than a million followers on Twitter, not to mention hosting a vlog and a podcast. He's even crossed over into mainstream media, having published five books and appeared on reality TV.

If your agency is run by an unstoppable Promoter, harness that big ego for good! Give them outlets through which to express themselves and be ready to field those inbound leads.

Communicators

Communicators have two special geniuses. The first is their ability to take complex ideas and boil them down into concepts that everyone can understand. The other is their ability to captivate a crowd.

They're your TED Talk-ers and keynote speakers. They're the charismatic ones that are perennially on the pitch team.

However, they probably don't have interest in one-on-one relationship-building or the patience for details, which is essential for sales. They're big-picture people who love to share their ideas.

An agency led by a Communicator is best served by getting that Communicator out on the speaking circuit and backing her up with a strong PR strategy.

---

[5] More about Gary Vaynerchuk and Vayner Media can be found here: https://www.garyvaynerchuk.com/ and here: https://vaynermedia.com/

Thinkers

Thinkers are the introverts of the bunch. They often share their talent for explaining complex ideas in simple ways with Communicators, but they're more patient with the details. They're the ones poring over the research as well as arriving at the big idea.

Where a Communicator is at ease speaking in front of a crowd, a Thinker is more comfortable writing a book or a white paper. Your new business strategy should support that. Give a Thinker the resources to write the book—and still back her up with a strong PR strategy.

You may have recognized yourself or others on your leadership team in these personalities. More likely, you to recognized most of the traits of one personality with a little of another mixed in (just because you're a Thinker doesn't mean you won't do well in a one-on-one sales situation).

Explore your agency's new business personality. You'll find it a valuable filter later when you are determining which new business tactics are going to be the most successful and sustainable for your agency over time.

7 IT'S NOT ABOUT YOU: DEFINING YOUR IDEAL CLIENT PROFILE

Once you've realized that narrowing your focus doesn't mean limiting your income, you need to figure out who, exactly, your best clients are.

A simple exercise that can reveal big insights is a client audit. Compile a list of current and recent clients and grade them based on your answers to these questions:

- Do they know they need the kind of help your agency provides?
- Do the recognize working with *you* is essential?
- Do they happily pay you what you are worth?
- Do they get great results?
- Do they provide great testimonials? Do they give you great work for your portfolio/case studies?
- Are they people you enjoy working with?

What you'll probably find is that few, if any, answer all questions in an overwhelmingly positive way. Even our best clients have flaws. Instead, you may see patterns that start to shape the definition of your ideal client.

The patterns may show consistencies in terms of:

- Client size
- Client team (in other words, the ranks or responsibilities of the people you tend to work most closely with)
- The kind of work you do most
- The kind of work that you enjoy most
- The kind of work you do that gets the best results

Approach this exercise with an open mind. It's easy to think you already know the answers to these questions – I know that was my reaction when I did this for myself, yet I was surprised by what it revealed.

For those agencies that are ready to approach business development in a new way, it may cause you to rethink who you sell to, which may also bring up a few of those fears I talked about earlier. It could also be liberating. You can shed all those unknowns.

The path to new business is not a well-lit one, but this exercise sharpens the illumination so you can see a little more clearly and a little farther ahead. Ideally, a set of patterns are revealed that can then be edited and arranged into a tight description of that ideal client.

Here's one more question to ask yourself:

- Are these kinds of clients easily identified and contacted?

An ideal client profile is of no use if it doesn't easily correspond to information in the public domain. It must be able to be carved up into terms that yield results when you type them into a Google search box.

This will help you stay out of the trap of relying too much on describing client types as "collaborative" or "respectful of the creative process."

No doubt these are qualities that you find in great clients, but they (or their opposites) are not easy to recognize until you start working with a them. It's easier to find social media managers at technology firms with revenues of $100 million or less, than to find a collaborative marketer who respects the creative process.

There's another reason why seeking clients based on softer qualities is misguided. It's all about what *you* need, not what they need.

They don't really care about what you need. A pitch written from that perspective will probably be ignored by them.

Prospects are more likely to respond if they recognize a bit of themselves in your pitch.

To illustrate that, let's go back to that agency I mentioned in chapter four with the tight yet descriptive positioning:

> *Strategic digital solutions for progressive nonprofits.*

Right off the bat, I know that if my business is not a nonprofit and I have no need for digital marketing help, this is probably not the agency for me.

The agency should see this not as a lost opportunity, but as time and energy saved. It avoided jumping through hoops unnecessarily to win me over when I was never right for them to begin with.

On the other hand, the right marketers will recognize themselves. In just six words, this agency does a great job at prequalifying its prospects.

Compare that with this from one of the other positioning statements I'd selected:

> *Our teams unite people, processes, and technology to create human-centered digital experiences.*

That statement is all about the agency, not the prospective client the agency is hoping to charm. While those "human-centered digital experiences" are crafted for the benefit of the agency's clients, the sentence is still forcing the reader to work way too hard to connect the dots to figure out if this describes them or not.

There's one more thing about the first positioning statement that makes it satisfying—that word *progressive*.

It's probably accurate for many, aspirational for some, but in general a positive attribute. I bet those nonprofits that see themselves in this word are proud of being progressive. It represents qualities and standards that have a daily effect on how they run their business.

In one simple word, the agency is making a subconscious connection with the right prospects: "yeah, these people are going to *get* me."

I don't have the benefit of knowing how that agency came up with this simple but effective positioning. Maybe it came to someone as they were walking the dog one morning. But I can tell you from my own experience that these kinds of simple, concise phrases are often the result of hours of thoughtful distillation.

So, where do you start?

First, you commit to making it about them, not you.

Next, crawl inside the client's head for a while.

What are the questions they're asking themselves that you can help them answer? What are the questions they don't even know they should be asking?

One technique for doing this is to think about their crisis moments.

What are the circumstances when things don't go as planned for them?

Or when they realize they're not equipped to face a new challenge?

What happens when their agency (the one that you'll replace) has let them down... again?

More importantly, what are they *feeling*?

Get into a quiet spot with your writing implements of choice. Think of that moment – the more specific the better – and start free writing, as though it were happening to you instead of your ideal client.

Remember, you (as the client) are probably not thinking,

> *"I must find a truly integrated partner who creates human-centered digital experiences."*

More likely, you're saying to yourself,

> *"If I can't bring this website in on time and on-budget, I'm going to be fired."*

As in the first exercise, see what patterns your free writing starts to reveal. (Or, for those of you who aren't writers, you might gather a colleague or two in a conference room with a white board and role play.)

Remember, this isn't going to be client-facing material, so get loose and be creative. Err on the side of outlandishness. You can always pull back.

When the portrait of your distressed client starts to emerge, identify where you can alleviate her problems.

Now, from this place of empathy and insight, write your positioning statement, or your sales email or your case study.

Just remember to keep it real—don't be tempted to fall back into agency-speak.

8 OPTIMIZING YOUR NEW BUSINESS ECOSYSTEM™

If you want a thriving new business practice that leads to healthy growth for your agency, you need to set up and maintain a New Business Ecosystem™ that's right for you.

An ecosystem describes any system or network of interconnecting and interacting parts. Ecosystems are dynamic entities and are controlled both by external and internal factors.

A New Business Ecosystem™ includes anything you would use to support the pursuit of agency growth, from a pricing proposal to a website to social media streams.

Like a natural ecosystem, it promotes growth. That is, as long as the interconnected parts are suitable for the environment and the external and internal factors are appropriate to their function.

Before you can design your ecosystem, you have to get some foundational elements in place. It's like building a house without a proper foundation. Sure, slapping together some sheets of plywood will get a roof over your head by nightfall, but it's not an effective or sustainable solution.

Your New Business Ecosystem™ will be in a better position to thrive if you can check the boxes on all those things I've talked about in the earlier chapters:

- You've committed to a market positioning specific to your expertise
- It's narrow enough to be operationally efficient
- You've confidently stepped into your role as an expert
- You've mastered your own story
- You know your new business strengths profile
- You have a deep understanding of your best client – who they are, how they can be reached, and the emotional triggers that signal when they need you

Bottom line: you must know what you're selling and who you're selling to before you can effectively figure out how you're selling it.

The Care and Feeding of Your New Business Ecosystem™

What I've learned from the small agencies I've worked with is that resources are in short supply. There's usually not the budget to hire a dedicated business development lead, and when there is, the person hired is often too experienced (and expensive), or too junior. In both cases, it results in dashed expectations all around.

Smaller agencies are often better served when they learn how to work well with what they've got.

That might manifest in a CEO that's on the road frequently to network with prospective clients, or a head of strategy with a polarizing idea that's expressed in a book or a podcast or a TED Talk—or a combination of all three. (In fact, it's the combinations that can be so catalytic—more on that in a moment).

It becomes crucial, then, for your agency leaders to know their new business strengths profiles (the four types defined in chapter 6: Hunter, Promoter, Communicator, Thinker).

When you can determine that with confidence, you'll be led to the right tactics and the right decisions around time management.

The New Business Ecosystem has four components:

1. Intellectual property

2. Marketing tools

3. Sales tools

4. Pitching tools

NEW BUSINESS ECOSYSTEM™

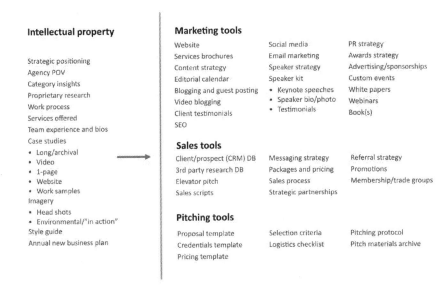

Intellectual property

Strategic positioning
Agency POV
Category insights
Proprietary research
Work process
Services offered
Team experience and bios
Case studies
- Long/archival
- Video
- 1-page
- Website
- Work samples
Imagery
- Head shots
- Environmental/"in action"
Style guide
Annual new business plan

Marketing tools

Website	Social media	PR strategy
Services brochures	Email marketing	Awards strategy
Content strategy	Speaker strategy	Advertising/sponsorships
Editorial calendar	Speaker kit	Custom events
Blogging and guest posting	• Keynote speeches	White papers
Video blogging	• Speaker bio/photo	Webinars
Client testimonials	• Testimonials	Book(s)
SEO		

Sales tools

Client/prospect (CRM) DB	Messaging strategy	Referral strategy
3rd party research DB	Packages and pricing	Promotions
Elevator pitch	Sales process	Membership/trade groups
Sales scripts	Strategic partnerships	

Pitching tools

Proposal template	Selection criteria	Pitching protocol
Credentials template	Logistics checklist	Pitch materials archive
Pricing template		

Intellectual Property

Intellectual property includes the basic building blocks of your original content. Sometimes you'll use these components in their original form but frequently you'll mold and adapt them for use in your marketing, sales and pitching tools.

IP should be watched over vigilantly and cared for diligently. Many of these elements won't need frequent updates, but it's a mistake to think you can create them once and use them forever. Make it a point to review things like your bios, photography, work process, and case studies on a regular basis (ideally once a quarter but no less than once a year) to make sure they're still current.

Marketing Tools

I've defined marketing tools broadly as anything that serves to create the brand persona of the agency, grow awareness, and support the sales.

For example, your agency's website or services brochures may play crucial roles in the sales function, but they're marketing tools first and foremost.

Sales Tools

The definition of sales tools is a bit narrower and refers to anything that directly and exclusively supports sales. Nevertheless, it's a diverse set of tools, encompassing the basics, like a customer relationship management (CRM) system and sales email templates, but also membership in associations for the purpose of networking and referral programs.

Pitching Tools

These are the tools deployed when you've converted a qualified lead into a real revenue opportunity. They support you in your quest to close a piece of business.

How to Create a New Business Ecosystem™ That's Right for You

If money, time and resources were no object, an agency would do it all. But that's not likely to be the case for your agency, so you need to choose the components that are right for you.

How do you know which ones are right?

- They align well with your agency's positioning (what you sell + who you sell it to)

- You have team members capable of creating, using, and maintaining the tools
- They align with the personality and strengths of the CEO or leader/leadership team that's been assigned primary responsibility for new business growth

Among smaller agencies in particular, I've found a few additional personality types that affect the proper functioning of the ecosystem:

Small Team Wearing Multiple Hats

This describes a lot of the agencies I work with. They have it tough because their resources are already overtaxed. They dream big, which means they set aspirational goals (to do any less would seem limiting and pessimistic, right?).

My suggestion to agencies in this category… be honest about the one or two things that your leadership team can do both consistently and well. Make a commitment to more achievable goals – it'll let you build momentum you can sustain over time.

"It's Your Job, Keep Us Out of It."

If the Small Team has it tough, these guys have it tougher. This category is filled with agencies that are fortunate to have a dedicated new business resource. But this poor person or team probably doesn't have the capacity to meet the truckload of expectations put on them by the rest of the agency.

If this describes you, my best piece of advice is to start looking for a better job at a different agency. In the meantime, be honest about the one or two things that *you* can do consistently and well.

CEO = Chief Sales Officer

Many agencies are led by CEOs who are better than any other team member at their agency at closing business. There are a number of reasons for this but here's a big one: the qualities that make them effective CEOs also make them effective salespeople.

The mistake some of these agencies make is trying to replicate that CEO's special sauce in other people, especially when hiring a new business person. It's never going to work so stop wasting your time trying. Instead, delegate as many other responsibilities that are reasonable to other executives so that the CEO can spend more time on growing the business. Tee up the ball so she can hit it well. Do what you need to keep her organized and on track.

Once you've defined the right new business ecosystem for your agency, make sure you have a plan for its long-term maintenance and health. Just like a natural ecosystem, you need to care for it so that it can support you. When it's working optimally, each component informs and enhances the other.

AN INTERVIEW WITH JODY SUTTER

Ashley Milne-Tyte, journalist and host of The Broad Experience, *a podcast on women, the workplace, and success, recently sat down with Jody Sutter, owner of* The Sutter Company, *to ask her about why she started her company and how she makes a positive impact on her ad agency clients.*

How long have you been doing what you do and how did you get to be a business development expert?

For most of my career I've been doing business development and marketing for creative services firms.

I started as a sales rep for a production company. I would literally "dial for dollars," calling up broadcast producers and creative directors at ad agencies all over the country and persuade them to hire one of our directors to shoot their next commercial (this was when broadcast TV was the most elite, broad-reaching medium your advertising money could buy).

It was super-competitive and my job could be grueling. But in hindsight, it taught me how to be resilient and persistent. And it taught me not to be afraid of selling. This made me extremely valuable years later when I started doing business development for ad agencies. More on that later...

When digital media became a thing, I wisely recognized the business potential and got hired by an early media start-up. It was incredible. We were literally writing the rules of online advertising. Advertisers were desperate to understand anything they could about these new media. It gave us access to the decision makers responsible for marketing at the world's biggest brands. I discovered a whole new aspect of advertising. Plus, I learned a lot more about pitching. Since we were pioneers in this new medium, we had few direct competitors, but we were selling against fear of the unknown! I learned how to educate my prospects and handle their objections, plus I developed a sense of showmanship.

This led to a stint working for several different digital firms, including what is now one of the biggest, R/GA. At the time, where I was part of a small core team that took the company from an unknown to an elite, sought-after agency.

By this time, I was a well-rounded sales executive, which afforded me an opportunity to work for a range of different creative firms – boutique graphic design firms, global ad agencies, media planning and buying agencies.

Having worked only for small firms at this point, I wanted to find out what it was like to work for a large ad agency. It was a whole new thing for me. I'd been used to doing everything myself at the start-ups and boutique firms I'd worked for in the past. Now, I was managing large pitch teams, sometimes spanning multiple countries. I became skilled at organizing and operations. I developed systems and tools to make our new business discipline efficient. Essentially, my job was to eliminate as much friction and chaos as possible to focus the team on winning.

To these big agencies, I was a rare find—thanks to all those early years dialing for dollars. It's ironic to me that many ad agency business development people have little to no sales experience—even though they're responsible for bringing in revenue.

When I started my own firm, my wide-ranging experience was really the thing that makes me valuable to my clients—I could help many kinds of agencies overcome their struggles with business development.

It also coincided with a lifestyle change. I'd decided to move from New York City, where I'd lived and worked for two decades, to East Hampton, one of the villages that comprise The Hamptons, the famous summer destination.

Thanks to technology and a growing acceptance for working with the best despite their location, I spend a lot of time serving my clients from my home office overlooking the harbor. But I also spend a lot of time on the road. There's still nothing like the productivity you get meeting with someone in-person, and I try to spend as much time visiting with my clients across the country.

Who are your clients exactly?

In the last couple of years, I've specialized my practice to work mainly with small agency CEOs who are underperforming when it comes to winning new business and would like to win consistently but also make the process less chaotic and exhausting for their teams.

Why the focus on CEOs?

Because, whether they know it or not, they are usually the best salespeople their agency has. I've developed programs that are easy for busy CEOs and their teams to embrace because they take both the CEO's strengths and the agency's available resources into consideration.

The agency business is so fragmented these days. What if you haven't yet worked with an agency in a specific discipline?

First, before I work with any new client, I give both of us a chance to assess whether it's going to be a productive relationship. If it's not a match, whether because I don't have experience in their field or for another reason, usually we both know after an initial "get acquainted" call. I'd rather refer a prospect to someone else than take on a project I'm not suited for.

Having said that, I've worked in or with so many different types of agencies and creative services firms that there are very few advertising disciplines that are unfamiliar to me.

Besides, the same good business development practices apply to any agency—and most agencies tend to make the same mistakes and struggle with the same challenges.

How are you different from other "business coaches?"

I don't advocate for just one solution. Some new business consultants take more of a "my way or the highway" approach—to work with them, you must buy into their solution, whether it's outbound prospecting or content marketing. In contrast, I believe the culture of the agency dictates the best approach.

This can be very reassuring to smaller agencies. Their resources are usually limited and the leaders, especially the CEO, have no choice but to wear different hats. It's going to require less of an investment and they are going to be more successful if I help them capitalize on their strengths instead of making up for their weaknesses. To take the hat metaphor one step further, I help them figure out which hats fit best and how to wear them.

In other words, if you've got a sales culture, then I'll work with you to develop a great outbound prospecting program. If you're driven by big ideas, then you're probably going to be more successful generating leads through a thought leadership campaign.

What type of personality do you work best with and what's expected of them?

It's less about personality and more about mindset. The most important thing is their commitment to making a change and doing the work that's necessary. I'm not a silver bullet! I make it easier by giving you structure and guidance, but you must be willing to do the work too.

However, I also recognize that every situation is different. Sometimes you're in a good position to dive in and devote a lot of energy to making positive changes. When time is not on your side, you don't want it to prevent you from seeking the help you need.

My programs were designed with that in mind. They range from coaching sessions, where we can zero-in on an immediate problem, discuss options for a solution, and decide on specific steps to address it, to a year-long New Business Masters program that addresses all components of a healthy new business practice.

For what type of agency is this program NOT going to work?

My approach is not going to work for the small agency CEO who contacts me saying, "I just need more leads" or "I just need to get more meetings with prospects."

First, more meetings aren't necessarily better if they're not with the right kinds of clients. Also, in my experience, a lack of new business meetings is usually a symptom of an underlying disease.

Once I probe a bit, I often find a slew of other problems that need to be addressed before the agency can easily get those desired meetings.

What do those problems tend to be?

Undifferentiated positioning, poorly defined target prospects, inconsistent and counterproductive marketing materials, and an inadequate approach to nurturing prospects, to name a few.

If I can't get them to see that these problems need to be solved before any kind of lead generation can be successful, then I'm not the consultant for them.

Also, in the rare cases that they do just need to generate more leads, then there are other firms that are much better suited to help them. I'm always happy to refer them to lead gen firms I like and trust and sometimes I'll even partner with those firms to offer a client a more complete solution.

What results do the agencies you work with typically see?

If they do the work, they close more business with the right kinds of clients. They can attract more inbound leads rather than enduring competitive pitches. And, when they do decide to take part in a competitive pitch, the process to be smoother and less chaotic because they'll have good tools and systems in place.

I got a call the other day from a client who told me that, because of the path I set him on, his agency grew revenue by 119% and saw a huge increase in profit from the same point last year.

Our work together got him to focus on pursuing the kinds of projects that would have the biggest impact on revenue and that strategy paid off.

When an agency is ready to work with you, what does that look like?

I offer four different programs:

1. New Business Masters – a year-long program that systematically improves all aspects of business development

2. Fast-track Audit – a one-day workshop that results in a plan an agency can implement itself

3. Pitch Fix – when an expert is needed to give an agency a competitive edge in a pitch situation

4. Individualized coaching – one-on-one sessions that address specific issues and get my clients focused on the right solution

I also work on a custom basis. Sometimes an agency is facing challenges that may not be completely addressed by the programs above. In that case, I design a custom program for them.

So, for agencies that are ready to get started with you, I imagine the first step is the get-acquainted call you mentioned, right?

That's exactly right. They can contact me through my website, www.thesuttercompany.com—they'll get a reply within one business day, or they can email me at jody@thesuttercompany.com

ABOUT THE AUTHOR

Jody Sutter is the owner of The Sutter Company, a new business consultancy that specializes in working with leadership at small agencies and creative services firms. She helps them identify and activate their natural talents for sales and marketing through programs that are easy to embrace because they take both the agency's strengths and available resources into consideration.

Before starting The Sutter Company, she ran business development teams at a range of advertising and creative services firms, from large global agencies to digital specialists. She was on the front lines, generating leads and building relationships that led to new revenue.

Jody knows first-hand what a challenge it can be to get the attention of new prospects and win the right kind of business for your agency. It takes hard work, creativity and discipline. But it can also take an outsider's perspective to help you understand your greatest strengths and how to position them.

Jody has tested techniques and tools designed specifically for small agency leaders that will get prospects to say "yes."

Learn more about The Sutter Company's programs and services at www.thesuttercompany.com.

Made in the USA
Coppell, TX
18 May 2021